HOW? WHO? WHAT? WHEN? WHERE? WHY?

ABOUT
SCIENCE

PUBLISHER	Joseph R. DeVarennes
PUBLICATION DIRECTOR	Kenneth H. Pearson
ADVISORS	Roger Aubin
	Robert Furlonger
EDITORIAL SUPERVISOR	Jocelyn Smyth
PRODUCTION MANAGER	Ernest Homewood

PRODUCTION ASSISTANTS

Martine Gingras   Kathy Kishimoto
Catherine Gordon   Peter Thomlison

CONTRIBUTORS

Alison Dickie   Nancy Prasad
Bill Ivy   Lois Rock
Jacqueline Kendel   Merebeth Switzer
Anne Langdon   Dave Taylor
Sheila Macdonald   Alison Tharen
Susan Marshall   Donna Thomson
Pamela Martin   Pam Young
Colin McCance

SENIOR EDITOR   Robin Rivers

EDITORS

Brian Cross   Ann Martin
Anne Louise Mahoney   Mayta Tannenbaum

PUBLICATION ADMINISTRATOR   Anna Good

ART AND DESIGN

Richard Comely   Ronald Migliore
Robert B. Curry   Penelope Moir
George Elliott   Marion Stuck
Marilyn James   Bill Suddick
Robert Johanssen   Sue Wilkinson

Canadian Cataloguing in Publication Data

Main entry under title:

Questions kids ask about science

(Questions kids ask ; 18)
ISBN 0-7172-2557-7

1. Science—Miscellanea—Juvenile literature.
2. Children's questions and answers.
I. Smyth, Jocelyn.   II. Comely, Richard.   III. Series.

Q163.Q47 1988   j500   C89-093167-4

Questions Kids Ask ... about SCIENCE

continued

How does an X-ray see inside you?

You know that light can shine through clear windows but not through a brick wall. X-rays travel in the same way as light; they can pass through some things but not others. X-rays are used to take photographs of the inside of people's bodies. Because bones show up very clearly, X-ray photographs are taken to find out if and where a bone has been broken.

Imagine that a doctor wants to photograph someone's arm. The arm is held in front of a piece of film. Then X-rays from an X-ray machine are directed at the arm. The X-rays "shine" through the flesh onto the film; those parts turn black. However, because X-rays cannot "shine" through bone, they do not get through to the film. Those areas of the film stay white.

The result is a photograph showing a dark shadow where the arm is, with the shape of the bones appearing in white. X-rays will pass through a break in the bone, making the fracture show up as a dark area on the film.

DID YOU KNOW . . . X-rays were discovered by Professor Wilhelm Konrad Roentgen in 1895. He called them X-rays because X means "unknown" and he did not really know what they were.

What do you hear when you hold a seashell to your ear?

Hold a seashell to your ear. What do you hear? The ocean? The wind?

It may sound like wind or waves, but what you are really hearing are faint sounds which are always around us but are too soft for us to hear. The seashell acts as a resonator—something that makes noises echo back and forth. This is mostly because of the shell's shape and smooth inner surface. When you hold the shell to your ear, it makes these very faint everyday sounds louder so that you can hear them.

If you were to hold a seashell to your ear in a soundproof room, you wouldn't hear anything because there would be no noises for the shell to pick up.

How do we hear sounds?

When you throw a stone into a pond, water ripples outward. When you speak, your voice acts on the air like the stone in the water; it causes a ripple effect that spreads outward. These ripples pass through the air and bump against a piece of tightly stretched skin just inside the ear called the ear drum. The vibrations then bump along the little bones inside the ear and send messages to the brain, which turns them into the sounds you can hear.

The ripples from low sounds travel further than those from high sounds. When thunder is close by, you hear the high sounds which are rather like the crack of a whip. When the thunder is far away, you hear only the low rumbles that travel a long way.

DID YOU KNOW . . . the squeaks that bats make are so high-pitched that humans can't hear them!

What causes echoes?

A long time ago people thought that echoes were little fairies who lived in caves and valleys. The fairies would shout back what someone yelled at them.

No one really knew what an echo was until we discovered that sound travels through the air in waves. When a wave of water is stopped by a cliff it is broken into a spray and thrown back into the sea. When sound waves are stopped by a wall, they're thrown back to our ears. Like the wave of water, the sound is shattered and comes back sounding faint and airy. It almost does sound like a little fairy calling back to us.

Why do socks get lost in the drier?

Fabric contains tiny particles called electrons. When clothes rub against each other for a while, some of these electrons are pulled into a special pattern. When they all line up in a certain way, they have an electrical charge something like a magnet. This is called static electricity.

In a clothes drier, clothes rub together as they twirl around. Static electricity builds up between them. Small items such as socks are attracted by this electrical force. They cling to other items where you may not notice them.

So check the dry laundry carefully before you give up on that lost sock. Otherwise, you may go out one day and find your friends laughing at the sock stuck to your sweater!

What causes electric shocks?

Water always flows downwards. So does electricity—it always wants to get to the ground. And just as water will overflow from a sink and spill downwards when the drain is clogged, extra electricity will spill over into whatever object will help it reach the ground most quickly. If you touch an object that is carrying an electrical current, such as an electrical wire, the electricity will overflow into you and rush through your body to the earth. You will feel this force as an electric shock. If a lot of electricity passes through at one time, it can burn or even kill you.

DID YOU KNOW . . . you sometimes get an electric shock getting out of a car because your clothes have been rubbing against the car seat and creating an electrical charge. When your feet touch the ground, the electricity rushes through you to the earth.

How is glass made?

If you have ever made candy, you know that you begin by heating sugar very gently until it melts into a thick, syrupy liquid. You have to heat this syrup to just the right temperature and then cool it quickly. You might pour it into a pan, or drop spoonfuls into cold water. The result is hard, clear sugar candy.

Glass is made in much the same way. Sand, soda and a chalky substance called lime are heated until they melt. The mixture is much hotter than the sugar you melt on your stove. Once it reaches the right temperature, it is cooled and shaped.

One clever way of cooling and shaping glass is to blow it. Glassblowers dip a hollow stick into the liquid glass and then blow through the stick so the glass inflates like bubble gum. If they blow carefully, they can shape elegant bottles and other objects.

How can a magnifying glass make fire?

You know how hot you get when you sit out in the sun. Imagine if the heat from the sun that was falling on one hand was put together and set on one spot on that same one hand. That sure would be hot! It would probably burn your hand. This is what a magnifying glass can do with the sun's rays.

A magnifying glass is made of one or two curved pieces of glass. When the light rays of the sun shine onto the glass, the curve of the glass bends them, changing their direction. It directs them all towards one point. All the heat from the light rays will be aimed towards this one spot.

If you put a piece of paper at the spot where all the sun's rays are being directed, a lot of heat will hit the paper. The paper will start to burn. Be careful if you try this experiment!

Why do you see yourself in the mirror?

A mirror is a smooth surface of glass that is coated on the back with a shiny metal such as silver or aluminum. The metal stops light from going through the glass. When light hits the glass, it's thrown back, or *reflected*. This is why what you see in a mirror is called a *reflection*.

When you stand in front of a mirror, light from the sun or a lamp reflects off your body, hits the mirror and is reflected back at you. What you see is a kind of "light picture," or image, of yourself.

But the image is reversed—that is, your right side and left side are switched. If you hold a piece of paper with writing on it in front of a mirror, you will see that the letters are backwards. In the same way, your image in the mirror is backwards.

Why do ice cubes float in water?

It's odd—ice cubes are made from water, so the two ought to have the same weight. If that is the case, why do ice cubes float in water?

Ice cubes float because when water freezes, the little "bits" of water, called molecules, push apart from each other. This means there is more space between the molecules in ice than there is in water, even though they are made of the same elements, hydrogen and oxygen.

This extra space between molecules makes a cube of ice weigh less than a cube of liquid water. Because it is lighter, the ice floats in water.

What happens to salt when you put it in water?

If you have ever put salt into water, you know that the salt quickly disappears. What happens is that the individual water molecules slip between the solid salt and break it up into tiny pieces. These small pieces fit between the water molecules. Scientists say that the water dissolves the salt.

If you boil the salt in water until the water evaporates, the salt will remain at the bottom of the pot.

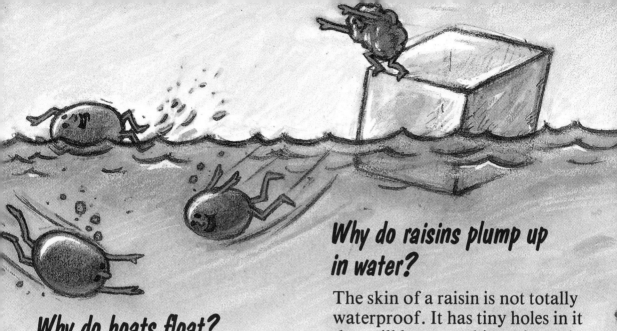

Why do boats float?

Take a knife and place it on top of the water in your kitchen sink. What happens? It sinks, of course.

Knives are made of steel, and so are ships. Why don't ships sink too? They would if they were solid steel like the knife, but they aren't. They are hollow and contain more air than anything else. All that air makes ships lighter than water overall, so they float on top of it.

Of course, you can keep on loading a ship until it becomes heavier than water. At that point, it will sink.

Why do raisins plump up in water?

The skin of a raisin is not totally waterproof. It has tiny holes in it that will let some things through. Water molecules are small enough to get through the holes. If you soak a raisin, the water will slip in through the holes and make the raisin swell.

You may wonder why the inside of the raisin doesn't slip out into the water instead! The reason is that the sugary substance inside the raisin is made up of molecules that are too large to slip through the holes.

The process that allows a liquid to be absorbed through skin is called osmosis.

DID YOU KNOW . . . some amphibians, such as frogs and salamanders, can absorb water through their skin by osmosis.

Is there a metal that can melt in your hand?

You know that ice and butter will melt in your hand—but a metal? Well, there is one. Gallium is a rare, bluish-white metal that was discovered in 1875 in the Pyrenees Mountains. It has an extremely low melting point of 29°C (84°F). That means it can melt in your hand—just from the heat of your body!

Why do magnets attract pins?

A magnet is a piece of metal which contains an electrical force that attracts other metals to it. Pins are made of steel, a metal that is easily attracted by this force.

When a pin is not near a magnet, all the little molecules that make it up are lying in all directions. When a magnet is near, the force from the magnet makes all the molecules in the pin line up in the same direction. As this happens, the magnet pulls the entire pin onto itself.

14

What is metal?

Everything that exists on earth is made up of different combinations of simple substances called elements. There are millions of different combinations, but only about 100 elements.

Scientists group the elements into metals and non-metals. Metals have certain characteristics that non-metals do not have. One characteristic of metals is that heat flows through them easily. You can test this at home. Find spoons that are made of different materials. Put them in a mug of hot water. After a minute, feel the handle of each spoon. The metal ones will be much hotter than the wood or plastic ones, which are non-metals.

DID YOU KNOW . . . the North Pole acts like a magnet. The compass needle points north because it is attracted by this huge magnet.

What is stainless steel?

Stainless steel is made with extra ingredients called alloys so that it will not rust or tarnish. It always stays strong and shiny.

There are 30 different types of stainless steel. They are prepared in different ways. Families use it because it doesn't need polishing, the way silver does. Hospitals, restaurants and factories use it because it's so strong. It is even used to make cars, planes and railroad cars!

The next time you're in the kitchen, look for some stainless steel. The sink, pots and pans, and knives and forks are probably made from this strong and shiny metal.

How can a submarine dive and then come up again?

A submarine can travel along the surface of the water, so it has to be able to float. To dive to the bottom of the ocean, it needs to become heavier.

A submarine has huge empty chambers, or rooms, in its base. When these chambers only have air in them, the submarine is light enough to float. If the submarine is to go underwater, the captain lets sea water into these chambers. Because water is heavier than air, the submarine sinks when the chambers are full of water.

Before the sub can resurface, the water must be pumped out of the chambers. It is replaced with compressed air, and the submarine becomes lighter and rises to the surface.

How does a periscope work?

A periscope is a tube that has two peepholes—one at the top, one at the bottom. Light shines in the top peephole and hits a mirror. This mirror is slanted so that it sends the reflection down to another mirror at the bottom of the tube. If you look through the bottom peephole which is opposite this second mirror, you'll see the picture that was reflected in the first mirror.

A periscope can be used to see over the heads of a crowd. You can hold the periscope so that its top mirror "sees" the scene just as a tall person would. The mirror sends the picture down to you, waiting at the lower mirror. You can also use a periscope to see around corners.

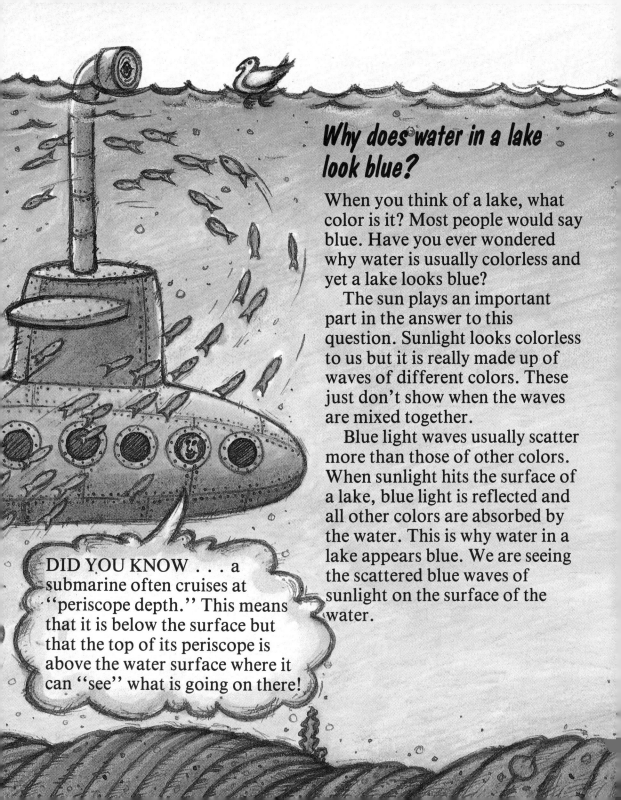

Why does water in a lake look blue?

When you think of a lake, what color is it? Most people would say blue. Have you ever wondered why water is usually colorless and yet a lake looks blue?

The sun plays an important part in the answer to this question. Sunlight looks colorless to us but it is really made up of waves of different colors. These just don't show when the waves are mixed together.

Blue light waves usually scatter more than those of other colors. When sunlight hits the surface of a lake, blue light is reflected and all other colors are absorbed by the water. This is why water in a lake appears blue. We are seeing the scattered blue waves of sunlight on the surface of the water.

DID YOU KNOW . . . a submarine often cruises at "periscope depth." This means that it is below the surface but that the top of its periscope is above the water surface where it can "see" what is going on there!

What is an element?

There are millions of different substances in the world. They may be soft or hard, rough or smooth, easy or difficult to break. Each substance is made up of different combinations of the world's basic "ingredients," called elements. About a hundred elements make up everything in the world.

Elements are pure substances: they cannot be broken down into simpler forms. No matter how you break it down, gold contains only gold.

Some other well-known elements are iron, uranium, silver, copper, nickel, mercury, aluminum, tin, lead, carbon, hydrogen and oxygen.

Substances that contain a mixture of elements are not "pure." Think of a cookie. Even the tiniest piece of cookie contains many ingredients: flour, sugar, egg and so on. Sugar itself is made of a mixture of three basic elements: carbon, hydrogen and oxygen.

DID YOU KNOW . . . a drop of water contains more than 33 billion billion molecules!

18

What is a molecule?

A molecule is not as small as an atom but it is still very, very small. In fact, a molecule is the tiniest particle of a substance that can exist by itself. If it was broken down any farther it would separate into atoms.

Molecules are made up of atoms arranged in special patterns. There may be as few as one atom in a molecule or over a thousand. For example, a single water molecule is made up of two atoms of hydrogen and one atom of oxygen, giving it a chemical formula of H_2O.

It may surprise you to learn that molecules are always moving. How fast the molecules are moving and how close they are together decides whether a substance is a solid, a liquid or a gas. In a solid, such as ice, the molecules are close together and moving slowly. The molecules in a gas, such as steam, move the fastest and are the farthest away from one another.

What is an atom?

An atom is the tiniest part of an element, and it has the same chemical properties as that element. Although atoms are small, scientists have discovered that their structure resembles our solar system. The nucleus at the center of the atom is like the sun; electrons travel in orbit around the nucleus the way the planets revolve around the sun.

The nucleus of an atom may be one single ball, called a proton, or it may be a collection of balls, called protons and neutrons.

Each type of atom contains a different number of electrons. There are always the same number of protons in the nucleus of an atom as there are electrons circling around it.

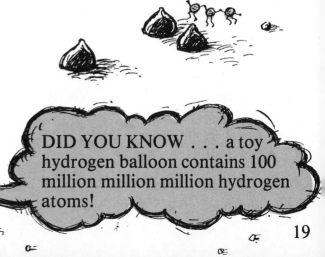

DID YOU KNOW . . . a toy hydrogen balloon contains 100 million million million hydrogen atoms!

What is a zeppelin?

A zeppelin is a huge airship that floats through the air like a ship floats on water. It can do this because it is filled with gas that is lighter than air. The German Count von Zeppelin devoted his life to the design and construction of these airships in the early 1900s, and they bear his name. There were other airships and other designers, but Zeppelin is the name that people remember.

His airship was a great frame of steel girders and braces that were covered with metal and contained large bags of hydrogen, another light gas. Engines with propellers and compartments for people or freight were underneath. A zeppelin could be as big as an ocean liner!

Zeppelins and other early airships had one great weakness. They were filled with hydrogen, which catches fire easily. When the passenger-filled *Hindenburg* burned in 1936, it seemed to mark the end of the era of zeppelins.

Today, smaller blimps filled with helium, a lighter-than-air gas that does not catch fire, are used for advertising.

DID YOU KNOW . . . parachutes have a small opening at the top so the air can escape. If they did not have this hole, they would travel sideways.

What is gravity?

Gravity is the pull that objects have on the objects around them. All objects have gravity, which means they are all trying to pull objects towards themselves.

The largest object on our earth *is* the earth itself! Because the earth is so large, its gravity has the strongest pull. When an apple falls off a tree, the apple pulls the earth toward itself just a tiny bit, but the earth pulls the apple much more strongly. Between the two of them, the apple ends up on the ground!

How does a parachute work?

A parachute shows quite clearly that not all objects fall at the same speed. A person wearing a parachute can jump from an airplane, open the parachute like a huge umbrella, and then fall to earth slowly and land safely.

What is stopping the parachute from falling quickly? The air that fills its huge canopy. This force is called air resistance.

How can computers be made so small?

Do you know what an abacus is? It is a simple instrument with rows of beads that move along a metal rod. An abacus helps people do arithmetic.

If you think of a computer as a very complicated electrical abacus, you will have a picture of electrical "beads" moving along electrical "rods" called circuits.

The first modern computers, made over 40 years ago, used bulky materials to make these circuits. As a result, the computers were huge—some were even bigger than a house.

Since then, people have discovered how to make the same circuits much smaller by carving little channels along tiny pieces of a substance called silicon. Tiny silicon chips make it possible to have very complex circuits inside small computers.

What is a computer bug?

Several years ago, computers were huge because of the bulky equipment needed to make them. Sometimes people found that their computer wasn't working properly. What was the problem? They looked inside to find out and guess what they found? A little insect had gotten caught in the circuit! Ever since that day, people who have a problem with a computer say there's a "bug" in it!

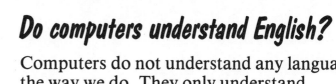

Do computers understand English?

Computers do not understand any language the way we do. They only understand numbers. If you press any key on a computer keyboard, the machine immediately turns it into a code made up of numbers. People who work with computers design them so that they understand these number codes and follow instructions. They also teach people which keys enter which codes into the computer.

For example, a computer can add two and two together if you press the right keys. If you also press the keys for the word "PRINT," the computer will print the answer.

DID YOU KNOW... the process of getting rid of the problems in computing is known as "debugging."

DID YOU KNOW . . . the number code used by computers consists of different combinations of 0 and 1. For example, A is 1100 0001. This type of code is called the binary code.

Who discovered that germs cause disease?

In 1860 a French scientist named Louis Pasteur was studying molds. He believed that they were caused by tiny living organisms that floated in the air, just waiting for a place to grow.

As he studied some of these tiny organisms, he realized they could infect cuts on people's skin and cause illnesses by growing inside people's bodies. The organisms were called germs.

Pasteur found that germs weakened and died if they were heated enough. He also succeeded in finding the germs that caused certain illnesses.

That's when he got the idea that made it possible to prevent some illnesses. He could weaken the germs and then use them as a *vaccine*—an injection that would produce a very mild form of the disease. The body would fight off the weak germs and would be prepared to fight off stronger germs it might get in the future.

Why do some people have allergies?

If a dog comes sniffing around, a mother cat might think the dog will hurt her kittens. She will try to fight it off because she thinks it is an enemy. A different cat, however, might know the dog was being friendly and simply ignore it. This example can help you understand allergies.

Allergic people have substances in their bodies that think other substances such as pollen, dust and fur are enemies. If one of these "enemy" substances gets near them, their bodies start fighting it. The fight causes unpleasant reactions, such as sneezing, a runny nose, or even a rash.

What is a zoologist?

A zoologist is a scientist who studies all aspects of the lives of such animals as birds, fish, insects, reptiles and mammals —including humans. Since there are enough books about animals to fill a whole library, most zoologists specialize in one area of animal study such as reproduction, environment, health, heredity, population, behavior or psychology.

One of the earliest classifications of animals is found in a Greek medical book which divided animals into groups according to whether people could eat them or not!

DID YOU KNOW . . . zoomania is a great love or fondness for animals and zoophobia is a great fear of animals. The word "zoo" comes from the Greek word for "animal."

How does a thermometer take your temperature?

When you have a fever, one of your parents may put a thermometer in your mouth to take your temperature. Most people have a temperature of 37°C (98.6°F). When you have a fever, your body temperature rises. The higher it is, the more dangerous the fever.

How does a thermometer work? Look closely at one. Inside the thermometer is a tube. The bottom of the tube, shaped like a bulb, is filled with mercury, a metal that is liquid at room temperature. Mercury expands, or increases in size, when heated. It contracts, or decreases in size, when cooled.

When the thermometer is in your mouth, the mercury heats up. If your body temperature is normal, the mercury expands until it reaches the line which marks 37°C (98.6° F). If your temperature is above normal, the mercury will continue to heat up and expand, and it will reach a higher point on the thermometer.

The clinical thermometer (the kind used for taking a person's temperature) is made so that the mercury remains at the highest temperature recorded. When your parent takes the thermometer from your mouth to read it, the mercury stays at the temperature that it recorded when it was in your mouth. Only when the thermometer is shaken will the mercury go back down the tube.

DID YOU KNOW . . . the word "thermometer" comes from the Greek words "thermos" meaning heat, and "meter" meaning measure.

How is frost formed?

Have you ever woken up on a very cold winter's morning to find frost on the inside of your window? Your parents probably told you that these exquisite designs that appeared like magic overnight were the work of Jack Frost. Unfortunately, the real explanation is not quite as magical.

Frost only forms when the temperature outside falls below freezing. The warm air of your room meets the very cold surface of your window, and the warm air cools. The cooler the air gets, the less moisture it can hold. When the air can hold no more water, the water vapor freezes directly into tiny ice crystals on the glass. The more water vapor that freezes, the more frost there is.

What is white gold?

Gold is a yellow-colored metal. So what is white gold? White gold looks like silver, but it is gold mixed with another metal such as nickel, silver or zinc. This blend of two metals is called an alloy.

Even yellow gold jewelry is made of an alloy since pure gold is very soft. Copper is added to make the gold harder and stronger.

Why use white gold? Although it looks like silver, it doesn't tarnish like silver. It is also stronger than yellow gold. For example, the claws that hold the diamond in a ring are usually made of white gold. The price of both types of gold is about the same, so you can choose which type of gold you wish to wear.

DID YOU KNOW . . . the proportion of gold in jewelry, whether white or yellow gold, is expressed in *carats*. Pure gold is 24-carat gold. Thus 10-carat gold is 10/24 or less than half pure gold.

Who said "Eureka!" and why?

Archimedes was a famous scientist and mathematician who lived 2200 years ago. One day, the king came to him with a problem. He had given his goldsmith some gold to make a crown. The crown had the same weight as the original gold, but the king suspected silver had been substituted for some gold.

First, Archimedes had to find the volume (the amount of space something occupies) of the crown. He knew that an ounce of silver would have more volume than an ounce of gold because gold is heavier than silver. So if there was silver in the crown, it would have a greater volume than if it was solid gold. But the crown's volume was too irregular to be measured.

Legend has it that Archimedes found the answer while taking a bath. As he stepped into the tub, filled to the brim with water, some of it spilled. He realized that the

28

volume of spilled water would equal the volume of his body. He shouted, "Eureka!" meaning "I have found it!"

Archimedes discovered the new crown displaced more water than an equal weight of gold—proving that the goldsmith had cheated the king.

What is fool's gold?

Many people have thought they've discovered gold only to find out they'd been fooled—by fool's gold. Fool's gold is made up of iron and sulfur pyrite. It is found in many places and looks like gold but has very little value.

To test whether you've found real gold, heat it. Real gold will melt into a puddle. Fool's gold will sizzle, smoke and smell bad. The bad smell comes from the sulfur.

DID YOU KNOW . . . some Indians used pyrite to make fires.

What makes a rocket go straight up?

An airplane moves along a runway and then slowly takes off into the air. Jet engines and the air rushing under the airplane's wings give the plane the lift it needs to fly.

A rocket does not work this way—its powerful engine sends it straight up into the air. The engine ejects gas at a supersonic speed, causing a chemical reaction. This pushes the rocket with as much force in the direction opposite to that of the gas.

Think of a balloon. If you let the air out of the mouth of a balloon, what happens? The action of the air escaping causes a reaction, and the balloon shoots off in the opposite direction.

On the launching pad, the rocket is pointed straight up into the air. The thrust from the engine lifts the rocket into the sky and above the atmosphere. Once the rocket is free from gravity, it will travel at the same speed in the same direction until it reaches its destination.

Why do some planes leave trails?

Most of us have seen a jet passing high overhead and leaving a white trail behind it. You have probably wondered just what this trail is made of and how it gets there.

Planes only leave trails in certain kinds of weather. The air that they travel through must be clear, cold and humid. Humid air contains lots of water vapor.

The engines of planes burn fuel to keep them going just the way cars do. When the fuel burns, it gives off water vapor. If the air is humid it can't hold any more water, so the water vapor condenses into water droplets. Because the air up high is cold, the water droplets freeze. And this is what we see, a trail of ice crystals.

Can jets fly faster than the speed of sound?

Yes, they can. But what is the speed of sound? Sounds travel in invisible waves, the way light does. Sometimes these waves travel very quickly and other times they move more slowly. At sea level, sound waves travel 331 metres (1,085 feet) per second. Some jets travel even faster than that. This is called flying at supersonic speed (*super* means "more than," *sonic* means "relating to sound").

This kind of jet creates shock waves in the air, one shock wave from the front of the plane and one from the back. A "sonic boom" happens when these shock waves collide in the air. The booming sound can be heard by people on the ground.

DID YOU KNOW . . . the speed of sound decreases at higher altitudes.

Index _____